Watery Worlds

RIVERS AND LAKES

Jinny Johnson

W
FRANKLIN WATTS
LONDON•SYDNEY

An Appleseed Editions book

First published in 2011 by Franklin Watts
338 Euston Road, London NW1 3BH

Franklin Watts Australia
Hachette Children's Books
Level 17/207 Kent St, Sydney, NSW 2000

© 2011 Appleseed Editions

Created by Appleseed Editions Ltd,
Well House, Friars Hill, Guestling,
East Sussex TN35 4ET

Designed by Hel James
Edited by Mary-Jane Wilkins
Picture research by Su Alexander

ISBN 978-1-4451-0376-1
Dewey Classification 577.6'4

A CIP catalogue for this book is available from the British Library.

Picture credits
Title page Pietus/Shutterstock; 2-3 SergeyIT/Shutterstock; 4 Pietus/Shutterstock;
5 John Goldstein/Shutterstock; 6-7 background Ishbuka Yalilfatar/Shutterstock;
6 Reinhard Dirscherl/Alamy; 7t FLPA/Alamy, b Amazon-Images/Alamy; 8-9 background Pietus/
Shutterstock; 8 Krasowit/Shutterstock; 9t Sarah Theophilus/Shutterstock, b Oksana.Perkins/
Shutterstock; 10-11 background SergeyIT; 10 Juniors Bildarchiv/Alamy; 11t AndreD/Shutterstock,
b Les Gibbon/Alamy; 12 AfriPics/Alamy; 13t Chris Hill/Shutterstock, b Orionmystery@flickr/
Shutterstock; 14-15 background Pietus/Shutterstock; 14 Photofish/Shutterstock; 15t Daniel
Borzynski/Alamy, b Picture Press/Alamy; 16-17 background SergeyIT/Shutterstock; 16 Derek
Croucher/Alamy; 17t Jozsef Szasz-Fabian/Shutterstock, b WitR/Shutterstock; 18-19 background
Geanina Bechea/Shutterstock; 18 Daniel Hebert/Shutterstock; 19t Christian Musat/Shutterstock,
b BogdanBoev/Shutterstock; 20-21 background Pietus/Shutterstock; 20 Jozef Sedmak/
Shutterstock; 21t Juniors Bildarchiv/Alamy, b Andreas G Karelias/Shutterstock;
22 Blickwinkel/Alamy; 23t Bruce Coleman Inc./Alamy, b Paul S Wolf/Shutterstock;
24-25 background Joseph Digrazia/Shutterstock; 24t Michael Ransburg/Shutterstock,
b Bob Byron/Shutterstock; 25t Koster/Shutterstock, b Roger de Montfort/Shutterstock;
26-27 background Andrei Rybachuk/Shutterstock; 26 Ivonne Wierink/Shutterstock;
27t Motorolka/Shutterstock, b Mogens Trolle/Shutterstock; 29 The Print Collector/Alamy;
30-31 Pietus/Shutterstock; 32-33 Ishbuka Yalilfatar
Front cover main image Hemera/Thinkstock, below left to right: Bob Byron/Shutterstock,
WitR/Shutterstock, AndreD/Shutterstock

Printed in Singapore

Franklin Watts is a division of Hachette Children's Books,
an Hachette UK company.
www.hachette.co.uk

Contents

Life in rivers and lakes

The water in rivers and many lakes is called fresh water because it is not salty like the water in the sea. Only about three per cent of all the world's water is fresh, but there's still plenty to fill long rivers and huge lakes.

A lake is a large area of still water. Lake water is usually fresh.

Amazing!

Nearly half (40 per cent) of all the kinds of fish in the world live in fresh water.

Rivers usually start high in the mountains and flow down to the sea or a lake. They grow bigger and bigger along the way. Lakes and ponds can form where there is a dip in the land so water collects, or when rivers meet something in their way. Most lakes are freshwater, but there are some salty lakes.

Streams are small waterways that usually flow into rivers.

WATCH OUT!
Rivers and lakes are being damaged by **pollution**. People dump **chemicals** and **waste** in the water and this makes it harder for plants and animals to live there.

River fish

There are fish in every type of freshwater home, from tiny ponds and streams to the deepest lakes and widest rivers. Some fish live in fast-flowing mountain streams. Others prefer slow-moving rivers and ponds with lots of plants. There are even fish that live in rivers inside caves.

A carp can grow to be 1.5 metres long. Carp live in lakes and slow-flowing rivers.

The world's tiniest fish is only 7.9 mm long – smaller than your fingernail. It is part of the carp family and lives in swamps in Indonesia.

Amazing!

Guess what?

The amazing archerfish catches insects by shooting them down from branches hanging over the water. The archerfish spits at its **prey**, knocking it off its perch into the water. The fish then snaps it up.

Fish called perch and many other freshwater fish feed on small water creatures and insect young. Some fish are hunters and they catch larger animals, such as frogs and tadpoles, as well as other fish. Piranhas are famous freshwater fish. They move in huge groups called schools and together they can eat animals much bigger than themselves.

Not all piranhas are hunters but the red-bellied piranha is a fierce predator.

A salmon's journey

Most fish live either in the sea or in fresh water. A few spend time in both salty and fresh water. Salmon hatch from eggs laid in rivers and spend the first year of their lives in the river.

As it grows, a salmon makes its way to the sea. It lives there for two or three years, feeding and growing bigger. When the salmon is ready to **breed**, it makes its way back to the river where it hatched.

Salmon may travel hundreds of kilometres from the sea to their birthplace. Some have to leap up waterfalls to get there.

Amazing!

This school of pink salmon are laying and fertilizing eggs in their breeding area.

The salmon does not feed on the way and the journey can be long and dangerous. When it reaches the river where it was born, the salmon **mates** and lays eggs. Most salmon then die.

WATCH OUT!

Salmon in some areas have difficult journeys back to the river where they were born because people have built dams across the river. The pollution in some rivers also makes it difficult for the salmon to survive.

Every year, brown bears gather by rivers to catch salmon as they swim upstream before breeding.

Nests and babies

Most sea-living fish leave their eggs in the sea to hatch on their own, but some freshwater fish look after their eggs better. One fish called the mouth-brooder keeps its eggs in its mouth until they hatch.

The labyrinth fish makes a nest of bubbles for its eggs. The bubbles are made strong by the male fish's spit. The female lays her eggs under the bubbles and her mate then guards them fiercely. The stickleback is another caring parent. The male makes a nest from water plants and the female lays her eggs inside it.

Amazing!

The mouth-brooder fish provides a home for its young even after they have hatched. If the little fish are in danger, they dash back to shelter in their parent's mouth.

Guess what?

The discus fish provides food for its newly-hatched young. The young feed on a sticky covering on the parent's body.

A male stickleback guards the eggs his mate has laid in his nest.

Crabs and other creatures

Crabs, snails and worms live in fresh water and in the sea. Water snails feed on plants, and freshwater mussels **filter** tiny bits of food from the water. Leeches are a type of freshwater worm. Most live by hunting other small creatures, but a few suck blood from much bigger animals.

Freshwater crabs help to keep rivers clean by feeding on fallen leaves and other waste. The crabs, in turn, are food for kingfishers and other birds, as well as otters and crocodiles.

A freshwater crab in an African stream.

A freshwater crayfish scurries over the riverbed as it searches for food.

WATCH OUT!

Most freshwater crabs need to live in very clean water so if you see lots of crabs in a river or lake that's a good sign. Many crabs are becoming rare because of dirty and polluted water.

Crayfish are related to crabs and look like little lobsters. They usually hide under rocks on the riverbed during the day and come out at night to eat snails and other small creatures.

Amazing!

If a freshwater flatworm is hurt it can split its body in half and grow each part again.

Some leeches attach themselves to their prey and suck out its body fluids.

Water insects

You might be surprised to hear that insects live in ponds and rivers. Some beetles and bugs spend their whole lives in water. The giant water bug is a strong swimmer and catches small fish and other creatures with its big front legs. The shiny whirligig beetle lives on the water surface and catches insects that fall into the water.

The whirligig beetle has unusual eyes. They are divided into two parts. With the top part the beetle sees above the water and with the lower half it sees below the surface at the same time.

Amazing!

A male giant water bug carries his mate's eggs on his back before they hatch.

Whirligig beetles get their name from their habit of swimming in circles.

Other kinds of insect lay their eggs in or near water. Mosquito eggs float in little groups on the surface or are attached to plants. Dragonflies lay their eggs near water and they hatch out into little swimming creatures called **nymphs**, which look very different from their parents.

A water spider with its diving bell.

Guess what?

There is a spider that lives in water. It makes a kind of underwater diving bell, which it fills with air bubbles that it brings down from the surface.

Frogs and newts

Frogs and newts belong to a group of animals called **amphibians**. They can live on land and in water. These animals breathe through their skin as well as with their lungs, but their skin must be damp for them to do this.

Most frogs and newts start their lives in water. The female lays her eggs in a pond or a quiet area of a river or stream. The eggs are inside clumps of jelly, which keeps them safe. They hatch into little swimming creatures called tadpoles.

Frog eggs hatch into tadpoles. Can you see the feathery gills that let them breathe in water?

Amazing!

A group of fish is called a school, but did you know that a group of frogs is called an army?

Many frogs have webbed back feet to help them swim.

Tadpoles have feathery strands on their heads called gills that help them to breathe in water. They also have tails to help them swim.

WATCH OUT!

Nearly a third of all kinds of frog and other amphibians are in danger of disappearing forever. Many have been killed by an **infectious disease**. Pollution and chemicals are making it difficult for others to survive.

The male great crested newt grows a jagged crest along his back in the breeding season.

Water birds

Lots of birds live in or near rivers and lakes and catch their food in the water. Long-legged storks, herons and egrets stand in shallow water, watching for fish and frogs. When one of these birds spots something to eat, it seizes it with its long sharp beak.

Ducks, geese and swans swim on the water and many dive beneath the surface to find food. They have strong webbed feet like little paddles which help them swim. These waterbirds eat plants as well as insects, worms and other small creatures.

This great blue heron has speared a catfish with its dagger-like beak.

Baby swans are called cygnets. They stay with their parents for four or five months.

Baby ducks can swim and find food for themselves the day after they hatch.

Amazing!

The white-throated dipper feeds on water insects and other small creatures.

Guess what?

The dipper is a little bird that lives by fast-moving rivers and streams. It does not have webbed feet but it walks right into the water and beneath the surface before starting to swim by beating its wings.

Turtles

Turtles have a heavy shell like a tortoise's shell, but they live in the water. A few very large turtles live in the sea, but most live in lakes, ponds and rivers. They are good swimmers – their legs are shaped like paddles for moving through the water.

Baby turtles usually eat insects and their young. As they grow, some turtles start to hunt fish and frogs, while others feed on water plants. Turtles spend most of their time in water but they have to come to the surface to breathe. They also lay their eggs on land.

Turtles sometimes like to bask in the sun on a floating log.

WATCH OUT!
Fast-moving boats are a danger to freshwater turtles. The animals can be hurt by the boat's **propellers** or hit as they lie basking at the water surface.

Amazing!

The alligator snapping turtle has its own way of fishing. Inside its mouth is a little bit of flesh that looks like a worm and the turtle wiggles this to attract fish. They come to take a look – thinking it is something tasty to eat. Then the turtle snaps up the fish in its strong jaws.

The red-eared turtle can grow to 30 centimetres long.

River reptiles

The anaconda kills its prey by squeezing it with the powerful coils of its body until it can no longer breathe.

The heaviest of all snakes spends most of its life in fresh water. The huge anaconda lives in the Amazon River, where it lies in wait for deer and alligators and other prey. The anaconda's eyes and nostrils are near the top of its head so the snake can see and breathe while lying in the water.

Amazing!

An anaconda can weigh up to 250 kilos. That's more than three grown people. It can swallow a whole deer or crocodile at one meal.

Lots of smaller snakes are good swimmers and spend time in water. The grass snake visits ponds, where it hunts for frogs and newts. The cottonmouth is a kind of viper and very poisonous. It hunts in water and eats frogs, fish and even birds.

Guess what?

The green basilisk lizard is a good swimmer, but it can also run very fast across the water for a short way, before sinking below the surface.

The water moccasin, or cottonmouth, is a very poisonous water snake. It hunts frogs, fish, birds and other snakes. Here it is eating a bullfrog.

Beavers

The beaver is a **mammal**, but it spends much of its life in water. Beaver families live in and around rivers and streams. They cut down trees with their sharp teeth to dam a stream and make a peaceful pond where they can build a home.

The beavers' home is called a lodge and they build it from branches and mud. The lodge is usually in the middle of a pond with an entrance under water.

Amazing!

The beaver has transparent **eyelids** so it can see underwater without damaging its eyes – a bit like having built-in goggles.

A beaver's teeth get worn down by chewing on wood, but they keep growing all through its life.

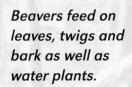
Beavers feed on leaves, twigs and bark as well as water plants.

The beaver family live in safety in their lodge. Beavers swim well and have webbed back feet and a paddle-shaped tail. They can stay under water for 15 minutes without taking a breath.

Guess what?
The muskrat is another mammal that lives near water and is a good swimmer. It has flaps that close off its nose and ears when it dives under water.

Freshwater plants

Plants such as reeds, bulrushes and wild iris grow alongside rivers and lakes. Water plants provide food and shelter for many river creatures.

The roots of water lilies grow in the riverbed, while their huge leaves and flowers float on the surface of the water.

Yellow irises grow best at the water's edge or in damp areas.

WATCH OUT!
Acid rain is polluted rain. When it falls on rivers and lakes it disturbs the balance of the water and makes it hard for plants and animals to live there.

Water lily leaves and flowers floating on the still waters of a pond.

Some giant water lilies have leaves that are two metres across. Duckweed plants live in still water in ponds or lakes. Each plant has a single tiny leaf, but they grow in huge numbers to make a mass like a green carpet on the water.

Amazing!

The jacana, also called the lily-trotter, is a bird with amazingly long toes. These spread its weight so it can walk on floating water lily leaves.

World rivers and lakes

Great Bear Lake

Great Slave Lake

Mackenzie

The Great Lakes

Mississippi/ Missouri

The Great Lakes

Lake Superior

Lake Huron

Lake Michigan

Lake Erie

Lake Ontario

Amazon

Nile

Congo

Lake Victoria
Lake Tanganyika

Ob'-Irtysh

Yenisey

Lena

Lake Baikal

Yellow

Mekong

Yangtze

The Nile in Africa and the Amazon in South America are the world's longest rivers. People used to think the Nile was slightly longer, but now most experts agree that the Amazon is the longest. The Amazon also carries more water than any other river.

Some of the world's longest rivers and largest freshwater lakes are shown on this map.

River and lake facts

The Amazon is 6,696 kilometres long and flows into the Atlantic Ocean.

The Nile is 6,650 kilometres long and flows into the Mediterranean Sea.

The Mississippi/Missouri is the longest river in North America at 6,275 kilometres.

The Yangtze is the longest river in Asia. It measures 6,300 kilometres.

The world's biggest freshwater lake is Lake Superior in North America. It covers 82,400 square kilometres – an area almost as big as Ireland.

Lake Baikal in Russia is the deepest of all freshwater lakes and has an average depth of 744 metres. It has more water than any other freshwater lake.

Henry Walter Bates was an English traveller and nature expert who set out in 1848 to explore the Amazon River. In this picture he is capturing an alligator with the help of some local people.

Watery words

acid rain
Rain that contains lots of acids. It is caused by the burning of coal, gas and oil which releases gases into the air. These mix with the rain droplets and fall as acid rain.

amphibian
A cold-blooded animal that can live in water and on land. Frogs, toads and newts are all amphibians.

bask
To lie in the sun or other warmth.

breed
To mate and produce young.

chemicals
Substances that are found in nature or made in a science laboratory. Some chemicals are dangerous and can harm living things.

filter
To strain from water.

gill
A part of the body that allows a fish or other creature to breathe in water.

infectious disease
An illness that spreads easily from animal to animal.

mammal
A warm-blooded animal, usually with four legs and some hair on its body. Female mammals feed their babies with milk from their own bodies. Cats, dogs and humans are all mammals.

mate
Male and female animals pair up, or mate, to produce young. An animal's partner is called its mate.

nymph
A young form of an insect such as a dragonfly.

pollution
Things that dirty or damage the natural world, such as litter and oil.

prey
An animal that is hunted and eaten by another animal.

propeller
A set of blades that spin round to make the boat move through the water.

swamp
An area of low wet ground.

transparent
A clear substance that you can see through.

waste
Something we throw away. Plant waste includes twigs, rotten fruit and dead leaves.

Index